THE LOST WORSHIPPER

The Pressures, Powers and Passions of a Worship Leader

ANDY D. SMITH

FOREWORD BY DR. JUDITH CHRISTIE-MCCALLISTER

ENDORSEMENTS

"The Lost Worshipper & Psalmist Andy leads the end time prophetic minstrel, psalmist, & dancer into a greater sense of conviction of who and whose they are & causes a deeper consciousness & awareness of who their gift and calling actually belong to! By so prophetically speaking to the modern day musician from the pages, an undeniable stirring is activated within the spirit of the reader to become the relevant, serious, souled out, & TRUE Worshipper God was and is still seeking according to his WORD! This is a must have for your spiritual library and will speak to generations to come!"

Prophetess Wosheka Jefferson-Burriel
Extreme Faith Worship Center- Pastor

It is absolutely imperative that every worship leader study the word of God. God has placed leaders, followers, and failures to go before us, so take advantage of every opportunity to learn from someone else's experiences & choices. The bible is the ultimate example we read about all of the failures and victories and apply them to our lives. Let this book serve as another tool that advance your knowledge in the worship lifestyle not just leading.

David Brinson
Faith World Church – Worship Pastor

The ministry and anointing of Psalmist Andy Smith can be described in two words: glory-laden and demon-chasing. Andy has the God-given sharpness and focus of a highly skilled warrior, a practitioner in the area of prophetic music ministry flows that open the heavens and exacts a divine sting upon those who encounter the glory of Jesus through the spiritual vocation of this man of God.

Prophetess Marcia Morrison, ChE, MBA
Morrison Ministries, North Brunswick, NJ

A must read for all Ministers of Music, Worship Leaders, Musicians, Pastors and anyone affiliated with a leadership role in any musical facet in the body of Christ. Psalmist Andy Smith challenges each of us to look within ourselves and become a catalyst for change so that true worship may go forth.

Minister Terrence Williams
Music Minister and Worship Leader
Zion Hill Church Family, Pineville, LA

This book is right on time! Psalmist Andy Smith has truly allowed God to speak through him to every minstrel and worship leader to do a personal and spiritual evaluation check. This is a must have book. Real. Challenging. Awakening. Inventory. Insightful. Powerful. That's what I describe this book as, in which I believe anyone that's in music ministry needs to have in their reference library. For the time is now for worship leaders to get back to the passion, commitment, godly character and the CALL they were given by God. This is the book to help guide you.

Elder Duane Terry
State Music President - La 1st Jurisdiction
COGIC
Lafayette LA

DEDICATION

To my Lord and Savior, Jesus Christ
My Brother. Intercessor, the source and
strength of my life. My life belongs to You
and I thank you for seeing me through every
trial, circumstance and challenge. You are
awesome in all of your ways.

This book is dedicated to some very
special people who were very
instrumental in my *PROCESS.*

If you could see me now, you would agree
that the fight for my destiny was worth it all.
Praying to meet you again in the
resurrection!

My Uncle, Tony Alphonso Jones
My Aunt, Connie Joe Smith

My Big Brother,
The Late Elder Gregory Keith Floyd
New Beginnings Worship Center

My Best Friend,
The Late Elder Jerry Wayne Hannon
Unity Church of God in Christ

TABLE OF CONTENTS

FOREWORD

I admire Psalmist Andy Smith for his courage in tackling, head on, a subject, which certainly needs to be dealt with in today's Music Ministries. Serving as President of the International Music Department for the Church of God in Christ Inc., affords me the opportunity to observe, first hand, just how much the enemy desires to keep those of us in the Levitical priesthood, in a state which totally contradicts the songs we minister.

In many "gospel circles", our music has become an "art form" depicting much of what takes place in the world, and in many instances pushing the envelope to buy into the shock value idiom to gain attention and notoriety from those who are not of the Kingdom.

Simply put – we must keep the main thing, the main thing! However, without an understanding of what *that* main thing really consists of, there is a natural propensity of declination towards those things that don't matter in the end.

In this writing, Smith disseminates to us some of the gems he has received in his various times of solitude with the Lord through him let us now hear what the Spirit is saying to us in this regard.

A village is sustained by its' water supply. Should the supply become contaminated, everything it touches becomes contaminated. As Ministers of Music, *(wherever your vineyard may be)* you are the water supply, purposed with the responsibility of bringing refreshment to the war weary soul...But how can you function in that capacity if you yourself are not healed, delivered and set free?

I encourage you dear reader to take your time with this book. Study it, ingest it and allow the Spirit of the Lord speak to you beyond the words printed on these pages. The Kingdom awaits you. Will you answer the call? Will you prepare yourself to be positioned as a trumpet, which will herald his Word? Now is the time and Minster Smith gives us an aspect of the blueprint for success. Onward and Upward!

Dr . Judith McAllister

Inheritance of Judah Ministries
Judah Music Inc.
President - International Music Department COGIC, Inc.

PREFACE

The book that you are about to read compiles a series of encounters that I have experienced throughout my years in ministry. Through this journey I've become an accomplished musician, worship leader, father and husband, and contrary to what people may say operating in leadership can sometimes lead you into some very compromising positions in life. In this book your eyes will be enlightened to a series of challenges that occur in the life of a worship leader. Sadly, many in this capacity have chosen to sweep such experiences under the rug.

The inspiration behind this project came from watching musicians, worship leaders, and choir members struggle with issues that nobody chose to deal with. They based this decision solely on the effect it may have on their individual reputation or the local assembly.

Oh, but thanks be unto God that causes us to triumph! There is hope and healing in the land of the living! Thankfully, we serve a God that's able to heal, deliver and set free. No longer do we have to worry about the opinions of people, but rather identify, face, and denounce the struggle that keeps us bound.

Dear Reader, you have been divinely set up! This book will strengthen your passion for the next dimension of progress in your ministry and life.

Ready, set, let's go…

~ Andy

CHAPTER ONE
THE FUNERAL SERVICE

Let us first begin our dialogue by asking this question. ***What does it mean to die?*** You might be wondering, what kind of way is that to open a book? Let me give you fair warning before you proceed with the remainder of this book. It is mandatory that you know in order to understand and receive the deliverance that will be offered through this assignment, you must first kill your agenda, your mindset, and your usual way of thinking!

The purpose of this assignment is not to hurt you but help you regain consciousness of your main priority. We have all experienced our share of tragedies and triumphs in the music ministry. Personally, I believe that it is time for us to finally become accountable to the mistakes that we have allowed to creep into the church and lower the standards of holiness.

One thing that the 21st century church has yet to experience in its entirety is the death walk. We have mastered conferences, seminars, etc. but when it comes down to us effectively communicating to the people how to maintain a spotless character we've failed. The only time the Body of Christ uses our lives as an example is when we have brought forth a reproach to the kingdom of God. Throughout this unfortunate tragedy, many in the music ministry are driven by the downfalls and exposures of others, causing an epidemic.

For if ye live after the flesh, ye shall die: but if ye through the Spirit do mortify the deeds of the body, ye shall live.

Romans 8:13
King James Version

In ministry, the opportunities that are awaiting us are on pause because of our lack of ability to re-align our will to the will of God. The enemy knows that if he can keep us bickering and fighting over small things we will never be able to focus on the things that really matter. So therefore, we remain in a stagnate and unproductive state. We must realize that in the Body of Christ, it is usually the small things that hinder our progress. Solomon makes it very clear to us that the issues that we have become so common to overlooking are the vineyard killers.

The bible declares:

Catch the foxes for us, the little foxes that are ruining the vineyards, while our vineyards are in blossom

Song of Solomon 2:15
NASB

It's the small foxes that keep up from being living examples of true holiness and righteousness. It will never be the will of God for us as worshipers to be disconnected from the vine. God has given us free will. We must want God more than breath itself.

Recently, I took the time to ask a few ministry leaders {Pastors} their personal strategies on how to deal a firm rod of correction from the pulpit. One answer stuck out to me, he responded :

"I have to be careful what I say because my people hang out with me so the closer they are the less I say"

...are you serious? So you're telling me that because you hang out with your leaders outside of the church, if you ever openly rebuke them you would risk the chance of them exposing you? But, sad to say, this is what the church has come to.

So as we travel together on this journey, please know that the intent of this book is meant not only to uncover and expose but bring healing back to the Body of Christ especially in the ministry of music.

The prayer of the worshiper should always be, "God, none of me, but all of thee". I often wonder how God feels when we present Him with our plans? The death of the flesh will probably be the most powerful battle of your Christian walk. *It never lets up!* When you think you've mastered one thing, another fleshly desire jumps up.

Many can testify that after putting Johnny on the altar, once you got him out of your system, you're walking through the mall, and all of a sudden, Ricky pops up? The flesh is constantly dying and it has to be crucified daily. The moment you think you have it all figured out, the enemy will set you up for the kill. You must walk in the spirit so you won't fulfill the lust of the flesh.

This is important particularly for worship leaders and minstrels because our field is a sensual one. *THE MUSIC WE MINISTER SHOULD NEVER MOVE OUR HIPS BEFORE IT MOVES OUR HEARTS!*

As worship leaders we must be very careful of how we stand when we minister. So many times worship leaders are singing, but the moves of the body are sending off a foul odor. I shouldn't be thinking about the club while I'm in praise and worship! Our obligation is to create a atmosphere where Heaven can kiss earth, not me kiss my ex in my mind. If we don't closely monitor our bands, you'll even here some R&B chords in the songs that they play. God is looking for a group of worshipers who don't mind dying to the flesh and allowing him to live in and through them. *Know ye not that your body is the temple of the Holy Ghost"?*

We must believe that if we are allowing things and people to share God's space we are out of His will.

You might be saying I am filled with the spirit and I pray everyday, but the Lord whom you give way to is the one that is in full control. Bitter and sweet water cannot come out of the same fountain. You can't lead me in worship and cuss me out after church. It's time to bring order back to the lives of God's people.

We have to die to our old way of doing things, and only then will we be able to see more of God through us, and His glory revealed. It's not that God doesn't want to use you; He is just letting you know that He will not use an unstable, double-minded, contaminated servant. You have to remember that you can be gifted and not be saved; you can be gifted and not anointed. What is the difference? <u>The anointing is the supernatural power of God on your natural life, which transforms your results from ordinary to extraordinary</u>.

I'll tell you what my biggest fear is...traveling around the country, ministering in song all these years, and in all of these different churches and get to judgment and the Lord says depart from me you worker of iniquity...I don't know you!

We spend so much time trying to get to "know" the wrong people; we miss all of the visitations from God that will make the difference in our life and ministry. We are so busy fulfilling the flesh desires, trying to make a dollar when if we would just apply the principle of Matthew 6:33 there would be no reason for us to be living in lack. You have to make a conscious decision that God will be the Lord of your life. He is not a man that He should lie, nor the son of man where he has to repent. Glory be to our God, if He said it...He is well able to perform it! I encourage you to begin denying yourself today, and allowing God to mold and shape you into a vessel of honor.

Put your seatbelts on because you're about to take the ride of your life. And we decree and declare once you have finished reading, you will find yourself whole and healed because of your ability to face who you really are and see yourself the way God sees you. Ready...set...let's go!

WHERE IS THE GLORY?

Have you ever wondered how it is possible to have worship services without God? Well as sad and as heartbreaking as it might be I must be honest with you...it is! Isn't it funny that God would provide us with a sanctuary to worship Him, the finances to upkeep His house, and still give us the choice whether we welcome Him or not?

He's the Creator of the universe, all-knowing, all-powerful, majestic Lord Jehovah, but he will allow us (His tenants) to be our own property managers. It is a proven fact that no one will ever appreciate your own things like you do.

Have you ever let someone use your car while you were out of town, and they knew that you were a clean person keeping things nice and neat? But when you get back drink cans, candy wrappers and food are all under the seat! Right then, you start feeling unappreciated and misused.

Why? because the person whom you loan one of your most valuable possessions to, has defiled your clean vehicle with unclean things. Personally, I believe God feels the same way when He gives us the opportunities to lead His people into His presence. Instead of being grateful we defile the atmosphere with our unclean and contaminated spirits! Our job as worship leaders is not to pollute the atmosphere with our personal feelings or agendas. It is an honor to be able to stand before God's people and lead them to their freedom, but allow me to pose this question, what about our deliverance? How long will our Pastors allow us to lead in ministry with dirty hands? The bible declares that Jesus is coming back for a spotless church.

I do believe in firm correction, however we have to be very careful how we choose to expose people. We are living in a time where even sinners have seen so many false people in the Body of Christ, where it has become rare to get a sinner to Christ.

Jesus makes a very revolutionary statement that speaks to the permanent success of the church. He says very plainly and effectively that if there is going to be a continual and consistent strengthening of the Body of Christ, here is the pattern

"And I, if I be lifted up from the earth, will draw
all men unto me.
John 12:32 King James Version

This statement has very little to do with our way of doing things. We must be honest and denounce the spirit that makes us think that our churches are packed out because of us. Jesus is the only way to God! It doesn't matter how well your administrative team is, how well you worship team ministers, or how well you can dissect a text...Jesus should always be at the center.

A lot of times instead of getting people to maintain a relationship with Jesus, we are spending time forcing them into a mold that is suitable and customized for our own personal need. We have become so discombobulated, that we don't even consider the fact that when people don't meet Jesus, they are in the church, serving you, and not getting any closer to heaven!

We have to get back to the basic, and that is first realizing that we don't have the power to change, save, heal, or deliver anyone. The Apostle Paul reminds us:

But by the grace of God I am what I am: and his grace which was bestowed upon me was not in vain; but I labored more abundantly than they all: yet not I, but the grace of God which was with me.

1 Corinthians 15:10

King James Version

So let this be a reminder that the power is not of us, but Him. God is looking for some people who are willing to lay down their personal agendas to accomplish the mission of the church, winning souls, empowering lives, and tearing Satan's kingdom down.

The father has reminded us through many situations in the word that, He will always have final victory! We must spend time in His word to find out what He said about life. It is a proven fact that if you surrender your life to God, He then becomes responsible for you. Like the artist penned so well..."my life is not my own, to You I belong, I give myself away".

Are you ready to experience a new life in Christ, a better way of living? Give your life to Him today! I want you to know from my personal experience, that He specializes in making something beautiful out of an ugly situation!

Will you choose Jesus today?

That he might present it to himself a glorious

church, not having spot, or wrinkle, or any such

thing; but that it should be holy and without

blemish.

Ephesians 5:27
King James Version

Listen to what the Message Bible says in
Isaiah 6:5-8

"Doom! It's Doomsday!

I'm as good as dead!

Every word I've ever spoken is tainted—

blasphemous even!

And the people I live with talk the same way,

using words that corrupt and desecrate.

And here I've looked God in the face!

The King! GOD-of-the-Angel-Armies!"

Then one of the angel-seraphs flew to me. He held

a live coal that he had taken with tongs from the

altar. He touched my mouth with the coal and

said,

"Look. This coal has touched your lips.

Gone your guilt,

your sins wiped out."

And then I heard the voice of the Master:

"Whom shall I send?

Who will go for us?"

I spoke up,

"I'll go.

Send me!"

I truly believe that a lot of our selfish ways of leading music ministries are fueled by our lack of consecration. It is impossible to introduce and get the people familiar with a God that you don't even know. Knowing God is to simply understanding the very *essence* of who he is.

The bible gives an interesting take on knowing God. The Glory of God has to be so important to us that we should be willing to give up anything or anyone that will hinder the power of God from being effective and evident in our lives.

Wherefore come out from among them, and be ye separate, saith the Lord, and touch not the unclean thing; and I will receive you.

2 Corinthians 6:17 King James Version

Hear me when I tell you this LOUD AND CLEAR: A church without the "Glory of God" is a church without a future.

God is not responsible for places where He is not allowed. If your church is not experiencing the latter rain of the Holy Spirit, you might want to begin seeking God, and see what it will take to get God in the house. Furthermore, you may seek to find a house where God is. He is near to those who call upon His name.

The LORD is nigh unto all them that call upon him, to all that call upon him in truth.

Psalms 145:18 King James Version

David said that my help is in the name of the Lord. Why not seek out the one who has all power and might? God is waiting to hear from you!

Our help is in the name of the LORD, who made heaven and earth.

Psalms 124:8 King James Version

For so long we have compromised the Glory of God because of denominational beliefs, opinions, and prejudices. It can be puzzling to understand how as a body of believers, we can eat the same food, put on our clothes the same way, be of the same Body, but get so many different interpretations of a very detailed book of instructions. I honestly believe that we are in a time where the Word of God has to come alive in our hearts. We need a move of God in the land today. Thankfully God the father has always given specific instructions on what it would take to get Him to move on our behalf.

Position, Prayer, and Progress are key elements, which will allow you to experience a Latter Glory Encounter. What are the requirements to position your church for the outpour of God's Glory? Come with me.

If my people which are called by my name will humble themselves and pray, seek my face and turn from their wicked ways, then will I hear from heaven forgive their sins and heal their land.

2 Chronicles 7:14 King James Version

- Relationship
- Humbleness
- Communication
- Desire
- Change

Jesus saith unto him, I am the way, the truth, and the life: no man cometh unto the Father, but by me.

John 14:6
King James Version

In a time where mothers are turning on daughters and fathers against sons, we must understand the importance of having a relationship with Jesus Christ.

Like the old hymn says *"be sure your anchor holds and grips the solid rock."* My brothers and sisters, not only is Jesus the way to the Father, He is the essence of being a new creation.

Therefore, if anyone is in Christ, he is a new creation. The old has passed away; behold, the new has come. All this is from God, who through Christ reconciled us to himself and gave us the ministry of reconciliation;

2 Corinthians 5:17-18
King James Version

It's in Him we live, move, and have our being. Many of you are wondering, what does being new creations have to do with being an effective worship leader? I'll tell you, "When you were conceived in your mother's womb, she did everything possible to make sure that when it was time to be born, you would know her voice.

You might not know how many times she rubbed her belly and talked to you during the 9 months, but she knew the importance of establishing a sound that no matter who was talking around you, you knew her voice. Jesus laid the same foundation:

Jesus answered, "I told you, but you don't believe. Everything I have done has been authorized by my Father, actions that speak louder than words.

You don't believe because you're not my sheep. My sheep recognize my voice. I know them, and they follow me. I give them real and eternal life. They are protected from the Destroyer for good. No one can steal them from out of my hand. The Father who put them under my care is so much greater than the Destroyer and Thief. No one could ever get them away from him. I and the Father are one heart and mind."

John 10:25-30
The Message Bible

Listen, Jesus said as I paraphrase, *"I don't know what y'all think is going on but look, I'm not out here on my own, I have authorization and legal access. The stuff you see me doing, is the proof you need to know that I've been sent by my Father, but I do understand that y'all don't believe me because you don't belong to me, the ones that belong to me, know my voice and are already PROTECTED from what's to come!"*

Aren't you glad that you made a decision to make Him your choice! Falling in love with Jesus was the best thing I've ever done. What a precious moment of celebration, understanding that not only do I love Jesus, but knowing He loves me too! As a matter of fact, He loved me first! Celebrate friends the ability to receive love! God has never vowed a promise without a covenant on your part.

"If ye be willing and obedient,
you shall eat the good of the land"
Isaiah 1:19

Seek ye first the kingdom of God and His righteousness and all these other things will be added unto you." Matthew 6:33

And there are many, many more. We as the Body of Christ must understand, the God is a God of order and He requires everything be done decent and in order. So as worship leaders and minstrels...our call is not just to sing the church into frenzy and leave them hyped up on emotional illusion.

The job of the worship leader is to be a testimony of the benefits that come with having a personal relationship with God. If you find me a church where the glory of God resides, I'll show you a church that spends quality time in communication with the God of Heaven. If there is ever a time where we need the glory in our churches, the time is now. We're in the midst of the greatest end-time revival that the world has ever seen.

And JUDAH...the frontline tribe has to be prepared to do whatever is necessary to plow up the ground so that God can do what He needs to do for, in and through His people. So whatever may be in our lives that will keep God from using us...today denounce, repent and return!

God has need of you; he is requiring a yielded vessel willing to be used! Are you ready to erase "ICHABOD" off the house where you worship, and your life? Ichabod stems beyond the church, it is any place where God was residing and all of a sudden, you no longer sense His presence or spirit.

But guess what...there is hope in your end! There is a chance for you to revive the glory that once rested on your ministry, in your home, and on your life.

A Declaration Over You

I speak over your life and ministry that every stench of Ichabod is erased from your life and from this moment forward you will have an uncontrollable desire for the glory of God. You will wake up wanting the glory, throughout the day praying for the glory, and go to bed resting in the Glory. May the spirit of God overshadow you as you walk this moment-by-moment journey called the death walk. The place where there is a continual battle with flesh vs. spirit. But greater is He that is in you than he that is in the world! Darwin Hobbs says it like this You're a Champion! So as you continue to crucify your flesh daily...remember that your purpose is far greater than the sacrifice of the flesh.

CHAPTER THREE
THE PROCESS BEGINS

In this life we were promised that man that is born of a woman is of a few days but full of trouble.

Job 14:1 King James Version

Exactly, what happens when our character doesn't line up with the anointing God has placed on our lives? How do we deal with the shame of being up one day and down the next? How do you cope when you find yourself in a prison situation, whether it be mental, physical, financial or emotional? Prisons are designed to isolate, depress and oppress. **Let me explain- Freedom doesn't come free!**

We have all found ourselves in a situation where we couldn't possibly see your way out. During these times you must trust and believe that God sees and he knows right where you are, and what you are going through. Depression comes to suppress faith and smother belief. There are times when your faith must be tested, tried, and proven. Allow me to be honest with you, there will be times where you will want to give up and throw in the towel.

The word of God the declares:

"be not weary in well doing for in DUE season, you shall reap if you faint not."

Galatians 6:9 King James Version

Faith without works is dead, so you have to do something...DON'T FAINT! You must do what it takes to set you affections on things above. To set in this context is not a spiritual term, but more natural.

You literally must take the spirit of your mind and place it on something positive while you are in the midst of your trial.

Set your affection on things above,
not on things on the earth.
Colossians 3:2
King James Version

Finally brethren, whatsoever things are true,
whatsoever things are honest, whatsoever things
are just, whatsoever things are pure, whatsoever
things are lovely, whatsoever things are of good
report; if there be any virtue, and if there be any
praise, think on these things.
Philippians 4:8 King James Version

It's amazing how the Apostle Paul knew so much about trials and tribulations. He disclosed exactly what it would take to survive. If the enemy can get any part of your mind, he will try to steal that very moment of peace and kill every inch of trust you have built in God. Today, I believe God is saying, "I won't put no more on you than you can bear".

I'm not saying this because I need words to fill a page, but please know that I am a living testimony of the keeping power of God!

I went through a few seasons in my life where I could not avoid being incarcerated. Yes, I was going to jail right in front of the church! It first began in my mind and then manifested in the physical. I don't care how long you have been locked away in your situation; I'm telling you that you can be FREE TODAY! You have to declare the word of God over your life and situation at all times.

God is not a man, that he should lie; neither the son of man, that he should repent: hath he said, and shall he not do it? or hath he spoken, and shall he not make it good?

Numbers 23:19
King James Version

The Example of Joseph

One of the greatest stories ever documented in the scripture is that of Joseph. The great thing about Joseph was when he was locked away, his gift never stopped working, God used him even the more! Being in a isolated situation has a tendency to bring the best out of you.

If your gift has not been tried, it cannot be trusted.

It is solely up to you how you decide to deal with the pressures of life and ministry. No matter how it looks or feels YOU CAN BE FREE! The enemy tells you that you can't survive this trial or you're going to die in this. You _can_ win the battle in and over your mind!

let this mind be in you that was also in Christ Jesus Philippians 2:5

What are you saying Psalmist? You have to do something you've never done, to get something you've never gotten.

When the Spirit led Jesus into the wilderness after fasting, every time the enemy tried to tempt him with something, JESUS USED THE WORD!

Notice here the bible never said Jesus left the wilderness to conquer the temptation. For those of you believing to be alone while going through, you now have more of a reason to celebrate. If you are going through, you have to sooner or later COME OUT! He defeated the enemy right in the midst of the storm. So I'm telling you that you can win this fight and begin again. Your life is not over because of this; this was designed so you could win! You're not supposed to lose.

God never called us to be comfortable, but he called us to be committed. Be encouraged and know that you are in the hands of The Almighty God. No weapon that is formed against you shall prosper. God has you right where He wants you to surrender. Don't ever think that God is not there, when you decide to praise Him.

In the middle of your test you will look up one day like I did and see the thing that you thought was going to take you out of the fight was only an illusion. A winner has been declared and it's YOU! The fight has already been fixed since Calvary, so yes; it's a done deal...YOU WIN!

God is so faithful that even when we sin, and turn our backs on Him, His love never changes. The bible declares whom the Lord loves he chastens.

So I'm here to tell you that just as you chastise your kids to help them understand your love for them, God also ordains trials, situations, and circumstances to show you yourself, when you get beside yourself.

The Spirit of Greed

I found myself one day, doing ministry, playing for major conferences, and doing what we call the "Lords' work." All along my heart was not pure and there was a spirit that had attached itself to my life, called GREED!

Greed is one of the worst spirits that has hit the body of Christ. It is the root of cheating, lying, stealing, and scheming. It was because of this issue that I refused to confront, that landed me behind bars.

Even though my sentence was not as longs as others, know that time doesn't matter when your future, character, and integrity is being jeopardized. Being on the frontline of the church as an accomplished minstrel, well-known worship leader, father and husband has its benefits as well as it burdens.

I knew what I was doing was wrong, but when you are allowed to minister without accountability, who's the judge? The enemy will never tell you that you are headed down a path of destruction.

He will never tell you that if you serve him, he will always make your way easy, why? Because there is no truth in him. Satan is the father of lies. Yet our God being all merciful, all powerful, loves us just enough to allow something to take place that will not kill us, but get our attention.

I must admit today that I wouldn't wish being locked away on my worst enemy. It is not the will of God. Yet through it all God will use whatever means are necessary to accomplish His plan for our life. I always wondered why God never forewarned Job that he was going to be picked out just to be picked on. The bible declares that Job was an upright man, but in a matter of minutes Jobs' life took a turn for the worse.

Let's take a look at Job 1. God has a conversation with Satan.

The Life of Job

Question #1? Why is God having a conversation with the one person whom He told us to resist? God poses the question, Satan where have you been? He replied going to and fro seeking for someone to trick! The interesting part was Satan never mentioned Job to God but it was the other way around. God asked Satan have you considered my servant Job.

Considered means to: "Think carefully about (something), typically before making a decision.

What words are coming out of Gods mouth to describe you? Can He trust you to stand in the midst of an adverse situation or will you do as Jobs' wife suggested...curse God and die. God's plan will supersede your expectations if you choose to endure. Sometimes standing means you will have to lose something.

Job lost his cattle, children and his servants, but the bible did not say Job wasn't affected by the transition. The word states that Job tore his robe and shaved his head and declared

Naked I came from my mother's womb, and naked shall I return. The Lord giveth and the Lord taketh, blessed be the name of the Lord. In all of this Job did not charge God for this wrong.

Job 1:21
King James Version

Understanding the plan of God or the way He thinks will forever be a mystery.

For my thoughts are not your thoughts, neither are your ways my ways, saith the LORD.
Isaiah 55:8

God is so sovereign that when He does decide to bless or curse, He doesn't consult anybody but the counsel of His own will. He discusses His plans for our life with Himself! What a mighty God we serve! The great thing about being in a pressured situation, is that God promised with the temptation, He would provide us with a way of escape. So even in trouble, God finds mercy necessary!

I was told once when I was young to always seek God in prayer and supplication because you never know when the enemy is trying to set a trap. Do you remember the old saying "everything that glitters isn't gold"? Well my father told me that everything that's dull isn't bad.

So many times we face situations where most people decide that since they weren't apart of the problem, they have free reign to walk away and judge. I am here to tell you from experience, being left alone to endure a trial, like being in prison is no joke. Sometimes you feel like the people you spent most of your time with on the outside should be there for you when you go in. I was always involved in ministry functions giving my time to others, and making sure their events were successful. But I had to learn the scripture that states put no trust in man the hard way!

I thank God for the visitors and letters that came, but they were not from the people I expected. But it taught me how to trust God on a whole new level. Faith is the only thing that will get God to move on your behalf. You have to trust God even when you cannot trace Him.

When I was told that I would need no less than $5k to put my feet on the ground and be released from jail I was ready to give in right then. I was already living from paycheck to paycheck, and on top of that I had no money on the books so where would I get $5k! But one thing I did have was my faith in God.

He begins to show Himself mighty on my behalf with no physical lawyer just the effectual, fervent prayers of the righteous. Many of you are saying now, "that sounds real good", but you don't get it. You will never know that God is all you need until God is all you've got. I found Him to be just who He said He would be, a fortress, deliverer, and refuge!

There wasn't anything I could do on the inside but believe God. Here is the awesome part, I knew in my mind that they were not false charges.. I was guilty! Have you ever been in a situation where you were guilty and God found you innocent anyway?

You know you wronged that person, you know you haven't always been faithful to God, but He decided to bless you despite of to show you, that it's better on His side! The bible declares that He would take your sins and remember them no more!

For I will be merciful to their unrighteousness, and their sins and their iniquities will I remember no more.
Hebrews 8:12

Even when man tries to resurrect something from your past, God has the slightest idea what they are talking about. Wouldn't we be in trouble if God decided today to give us our recompense reward for the things we have done? Who would be able to stand? Through this I experienced the immeasurable forgiving power of God as well as His unmerited favor. Just like David in Psalms 51, he knew what he had done was wrong in the eyesight of God, and the problem lies here. Many of us commit sin and feel like we are justified in the reason why we did what we did.

We are walking around with un-repented sin in our lives but expecting miracles, signs, and wonders. When I rededicated my life back to God, all of a sudden I began to see the miracle power of God working on my behalf. Shortly thereafter, I heard of two Pastors in my city raising funds to help with my being released! Glory Be Unto God!

God does not look at the outer appearance but He only sees the heart. When your heart is right before God, and your ways please the Lord, he'll make even your enemies be at peace with you. The older saints use to tell us, never burn your bridges because you never know when you have to cross them again. I'm standing as a testimony to tell you that God took my personal circumstance and provoked my passion and begin to call forth productivity.

Here I am today healed, delivered, and free.

To God be the Glory!

I returned, and saw under the sun, that the race is not to the swift, nor the battle to the strong, neither yet bread to the wise, nor yet riches to men of understanding, nor yet favour to men of skill; but time and chance happeneth to them all.

Ecclesiastes 9:11

Don't ever think that the pressure that you are put under because of your anointing is always the enemy. God will order and orchestrate the perfect situation, just to see if you will trust and praise Him while He is working on your behalf.

Perhaps your pressures may be inside the church, in a relationship that has you entangled mentally. May I suggest to you today, that just by the mere fact that you are reading this book you are one step closer to your deliverance? You can be free today from the spirits that have you bound!

Whether it is depression, oppression, low self-esteem, malice, witchcraft, pornography, sexual immorality, or just abuse, misuse or lack of trust. You can be made whole right now at this very moment by confessing you have a problem. You will never conquer what you are not able to confront.

Ask God to shine the light of the Spirit on every hidden thing. This is a must before you begin to uncover the issues that hold you captive. Then and only then will you receive freedom from that thing.

Have you ever noticed that in the midst of the worst seasons of your life, that's when God uses you the most? Why? Because *you're empty, weak, and available! And he said unto me, My grace is sufficient for thee: for my* strength is made perfect in weakness 2 Corinthians 12:9.

God understands that while we are going through, we become more alert to everything that we do. God also knows that for some of us, the only time He can get our attention is through a storm! I admit that was me!

I was one of the ones who would only talk to God on Sundays, and when I needed Him! I guess we think God is retarded or something. Just because He comes through on our behalf, doesn't mean that we have mastered manipulating Him! DON'T BE CRAZY!

God is all knowing! So before you think your thought, He knows it. We have to learn that God requires truth from the inward part. What does it profit you holding information from God that He already knows? God wants to hear you confess your faults, and He said it...He would be faithful and just to forgive you! It doesn't hurt your enemy when you walk around with un-repented sin in your life. It hurts you! If most people understood that walking around with pride and arrogance only shows your low level of maturity. As worship you must be able to keep your hearts pure. How can you release life into an atmosphere, when your life is locked up with un-forgiveness and bitterness?

Now, please understand that there is a huge difference between singing your way out of sin and singing while in sin! I have seen many worship leaders sing their way into deliverance because number one...THEY WANTED IT!

We are living in such a day where, worship leaders, minstrels, pastors, etc. would rather risk the chance of God exposing them in public, than getting it right in the prayer closet. What you do in private, I promise you God will reward you openly. And right now I want to take authority of the spirit of pride that causes you to purposely make you feel like you're right in your wrong! I decree and declare that humbleness and humility shall lead your ministry.

I declare over your life worshiper, that every time God shows you that there is a piece of pride trying to rise up in your life, you will stop what you are doing and deal with it!

I declare over your life that you have live in total peace and your ministry shall operate in purity and meekness. In Jesus' name, Amen! We must understand that God is a God that deals with the intentions of a mans heart. Even though he hates the sin, God love the sinner. It is His will that we minister through song healed and whole. It is much easier to win a soul by example.

The life of a worship leader is not suppose to be complex, confusing, or corrupt. As a worship leader, we must no deny the fact that pain and pressure are a vital part of our making. Contrary to popular belief, the anointing never goes on sale neither does it come half off?

Even though Jesus knew that He about to die, his humanistic nature became obvious in the Garden of Gethsemane.

Father, if thou be willing, remove this cup from me: nevertheless not my will, but thine, be done.
Luke 22:42

Now let's turn a curve, expose the *pressures* that are usually placed on worship leaders. Buckle Up! There will be al lot of instances where, we will ask God why do I have to go through this. But you must understand, that God always knows what's in us. If you're going to ever be anything great in God, we must understand that drinking the cup of suffering is inevitable. There will be times where God doesn't say anything to us, but He's there. I'm not too fond of those times, because the outcome of your trial is solely based upon your faith. Every man is giving a measure, but if you ever want to build your faith, get in a situation where if God doesn't come through you won't come out!

I'm telling you my brothers and sisters, God knows exactly what it will take to get the yes out of us. But I'm so glad there was a song penned "trouble don't last always". Don't fight the process of your anointing, it's like fine meat, sometimes it has to be processed more times than the average meat.

God is a Refiner all by Himself. And to be totally honest, shedding tears doesn't bring the trial to close any sooner, begging God doesn't either! Job lost everything He had, and he was upright and he still had to pay full price but in the end, it was rewarded to Job double for His trouble. Case closed!

CHAPTER FOUR
ACCOUNTABILITY

As worship leaders it is quite often said that to be called to the ministry of worship you had to be three things: loyal, patient, and gifted. In order to serve as a leader in the local church you had to be loyal to the Pastor, the church and the worship team. Patience was also a factor as a work in progress.

We've all heard the saying, "God is not through with me yet". This cliché has simply made premature excuses, which were free rights to live a nasty life. We were often told that we had to be gifted for the task at hand. They would repeatedly remind us that this is a ministry of integrity, and we want to always put our best foot forward so we won't embarrass the church, the pastors, or God. Yes I have heard it all!

From the perception of a person who was seeking a place to be accepted, affirmed, and validated, that all sounded wonderful. Take this story for example. We would like to welcome Minister Andy Smith to First Brighter Day Grapefruit Church. He is our new Worship Pastor and will be assuming leadership of the music ministry as of this week.

In the meantime, the person that is over the worship team now hasn't been told anything, which brings me to my first point:

The Curse of No Communication:

What would happen to our music ministries if we begin talking things out instead of taking things personal? I have found out that the biggest problem that will ever arise in the music ministry is when identity is misunderstood. The enemy always throws his strongest blow through communication.

"Whatever isn't revealed, produces strength to kill."

The relationships within the music ministry should not be limited to the Pastor/ Music Minister.

What about the band? So many times we just limit the band to being gifted and not caring whether their souls went to hell or heaven. For instance, what if the drummer has something, going on in his life and the only time he receives communication is when he is asked to learn a song. Yet because he feels like he can't talk to anyone, he commits suicide. WOW! Who do we blame - the devil?

There is a need to invest and hire skillful minstrels and worship leaders, those who can hear God. Additionally they are to ensure that they are in tune with the spirit to know when something is wrong with one of the team members.

A Note to Ministry Leaders

Please be aware of the spirit that will come in to separate the team. It is vitally important that we make sure there is always an open line of communication between every member that makes up the team.

I am sympathetic to the lack of flow existent in our services. Throughout my tenure, traveling across the country conducting workshops and seminars, and upon my arrival I was informed by the Pastor that the church has a great band but they are not tapping into the flow.

Why aren't they producing? As the workshop begins, it is usually by the end of the first session, that shows there is a problem between leadership. You will most commonly find the issue between the minister of music and worship leader. The workshop that was meant to be a time of impartation and refreshing, has turned into a time of revealing un-forgiveness and offenses.

How can you deal with things that are stopping the progress of ministry if it is never brought to exposure. For years we have heard un-wise counsel and were told to "pray about it". My philosophy is simple, "pray about it and then share it to fix it!

"If my job is to make sure the worship service is in order and the God of the earth is pleased with our worship, the only way I can be effective is to make sure my heart is pure towards God and His people. The line of communication does not mean that when your team confides in you, you take their business to the street. I believe this is one of the reasons why God cannot trust us with national influence because our ability to handle our local assignment is tainted. We must be leaders that can be trusted with the pain and secrets of others.

Many people leave ministries because they expect out of leadership what was never suppose to be a requirement. By all means, if you find someone in the church that you can share your problems with and they have proven to be trustworthy, cherish the relationship. Don't get all bent out of shape if you take your business to a person that is first of all, out of alignment with the church themselves!

However, it would help in most situations if we would ask God for discernment before we opened up the gates of our heart. I am a living witness that their is no struggle, situation or problem, God doesn't cover in His word. It is amazing how we will run to people before we run to God. I can truly say I was once guilty of that, seeking counsel from people who were wrapped up in problems themselves.

Communication amongst the family is supposed to be an instrument of healing and restoration when trouble arises. But then you have those "Absalom's"...who are patiently waiting at the door to take the weaknesses of the ministry to the enemy's camp! Discernment is a vital gift to have in these last and evil days!

The Curse Of A Nasty Life.

Many times as worship leaders and ministers we become so busy trying to fulfill responsibilities, we forget about purifying our own lives. However, we cannot forget that we came to the ministry broken and full of hell.

Sadly, because we were gifted, speaking in tongues, and had a reputation the leaders put us right into position without finding out who we really were. They didn't know that you were put out of the last church brother musician, for having babies all of the church, and sister worship leader for having illicit relationship with the same sex and refused the help to be delivered!

Subsequently, the spirit that we operated in at our previous ministry has begun to attach itself to people in the new church. Now the Pastor is wondering why Sis. Sally is changing. She use to be faithful, and now she's short when you talk to her, missing bible study, but people have spotted her throughout the city hanging with the worship leader, Everything has changed! A lot of our worship leaders are *"leading while bleeding"*. Usually when you hear this statement, you immediately think about pain and un-resolved issues from Pastors, but what about leading while bleeding "contaminated character"?

The cliché says "the birds of a feather, flock together". So many times we misuse the Grace of God for an escape route. But the bible says that *"should we continue in sin that grace may abound"?*

We must have the sense enough to know when we are infected and when we are infecting others with the dis-ease of slothfulness, sin, and lack of accountability.

It is very easy to spot when a person has been affected by a spirit not of God, everything about their personality changes. The most common form where you can spot this issue is when a single person sold out to the Lord starts dating. If dating changes the way you serve the church, then maybe you're dating prematurely.

Scripture states that *"the blessings of the Lord maketh rich and add no sorrow."* God is a God of order and excellence. He will not lead you into any sin, or any compromising situations. So we must be careful of the company we surround ourselves with.

The bible declares in *Hebrews 12:1 that we need to lay aside every sin and weight that so easily besets us.* For the self-righteous saints that believe that they are living holy to the Lord, and that's great...but what about your nasty attitude or the fact that you're dating a unbeliever?

You may be asking the question, how do we fix the issue? The answer is quite simple: *repair, restore, and revive your passion for Holiness!* Take the necessary time in the presence of the Lord, to find out what God is saying about your life and ministry. Prayer is the essential key to the success of any ministry. You can't go around trying to shift atmospheres and you don't even know if God is standing with you or not. Communicate with Him, get to know Him, as a matter of fact allow yourself to be lost in His presence. Let your daily prayer be, God, I'm lost without You. I don't know about you but I have the sense of know that accountability doesn't stop with the Pastors of your church. You are accountable to God first!

He is the one who called you, so why would you seek the approval of man, before the man who gave you the opportunity. So I admonish you today to get in the word! Study the word! Meditate on the word! Let the word of God be your daily bread and I promise you, your life and ministry will grow to levels unknown!

So as you journey as a minstrel, worship leader etc., please know that God has your back, and no matter the situation. YOU CAN WIN! You were never created to allow situation and circumstances to dictate your growth in the Kingdom. Knowledge is Power! Allow God to prepare you for what you have been predestined for. Greater is ahead!

CHAPTER FIVE
THE DECEITFUL PASSION OF AFFIRMATION

"Don't Give Them Too Much Too Soon"

As we progress to this chapter, please understand that we have come to a very important crossroad. Your response to this chapter will ultimately determine where you stand when it comes to a particular issue that most pastors, minstrels, and worship leaders never uncover. It's a dangerous subject, but yet a subject that needs to be discussed. I believe that every person in ministry has needed this form of validation at least once in their lifetime. We are living in a day and time where there are so many changes that are taking place in the Body of Christ. If I had to make a common declaration it would be simply be this, we are living in the last days! It is no secret that at least 65% of people in ministry are in it for the wrong reasons.

You may be asking, what is the easiest way to know if a person has ulterior motives when they come to a ministry? The answer is this- *keep your eyes on anyone that makes it their goal and main purpose to get next to the Pastor{s} and/or Leadership.*

One of the things that has changed drastically from the days of old is before leaders accepted members into their congregation especially from a church that everyone knew; they would call the former Pastor to find out what caused that member to leave. When you open up your doors to people without knowing why they are there, you are subject to having a mess on your hands.

Understand that I am in no ways telling you that people don't get hurt in church and need restoration and healing, etc. I am saying this; you must be careful in ministry because a lot of churches do not fellowship because of the mess that is kept up between lay members.

One thing I learned at a very young age is ministry was LOYALTY. Why attach yourself to a ministry that you don't even believe in? Personally, I believe that we are in an hour where God is about to uncover the deceitful passions that are hidden in our assemblies. We have a plethora of leaders serving with ulterior motives and we as the Body, are sitting by and allowing this spirit to hinder the progress of the Lord's church. We are held accountable for every deed done in this body. We need to go back to the altar and ask God to give us our eyes back, where we can see the enemy coming from afar.

Churches are falling apart because we have leaders that are being *"held hostage"* by spiritual terrorists. Some Pastors may be saying right now, I have full control over everything that goes on in my church, and what I say is law. Well let's see!

Let's take a closer and in-depth look at the word terrorism: *[ter-uh-riz-uhm]*

The use of violence and threats to intimidate or coerce, especially for political purposes. The state of <u>fear</u> and submission produced by terrorism or <u>terrorization</u>. A terroristic method of governing or of resisting a government

Okay, so it's just this simple…your musician isn't faithful, doesn't have a desire to see the church excel to its highest potential, but you keep them because your pews are filled! You are sacrificing progress for position! Have you ever been told that if you don't do this or do that, "I'm leaving"?

The greatest test of any leader is making the decision that affects the church but frees the church at the same time. We as minstrels have been guilty of operating out of obligation for so long, that when we truly decide to commit whole-heartedly to the work, it's difficult because we're not taken seriously.

God wants tc deliver us from people who feel as if the ministry can't go on without them because of the role they play in the church. I am a firm believer that if your church is pleasing God, there will never be any lack. However, just like in any movie or stage play, scenes change.

My fellow brothers and sisters being used in the capacity of worship leaders and musicians, be very careful of holding Gods leaders hostage. You will wake up one day very soon and realize that you have been replaced, not by man, but by God, our heavenly father. Serve your local church with a pure and humble spirit. Faithfulness has its own reward!

If you have noticed, the church has taken the innocence and purity out of affirmation and validation. I know everybody has heard the saying "I don't need anybody to validate me", and usually it comes from the people who need it the most.

Now, this chapter is going to be a little more demanding because it should cause you to look back over your life and see where you have made certain decisions because of passions that were misunderstood and misplaced. We all have made mistakes in the past and we are consistently seeing evidence that some issues are not dead just lying dormant.

As we delve deeper into this topic of "the deceitful passion of affirmation" understand that our main focus is to expose the secrets of the flesh. According to Romans 8:7, the flesh is enmity to God. Then we flip over to Jeremiah 17:9 to hear the word of God say " the heart is desperately wicked who can know it" I will pose this question, what's in my heart that causes me to "demand" affirmation?

Do you think it's wise to stand before God's people portraying a particular anointing yet when the opportunity arises for you to operate in the realm that you so boastfully pride yourself in, you fail?

Again, stay in your lane. God has given us leaders for a reason. I have seen in many worship services where the worship team could not press through, the worship leaders could not break the house. Recently, on a Sunday morning one of our Senior Pastors gave us some powerful revelation on rank in the spirit. So, we left rehearsal feeling like "power rangers"! We knew that we were prepared for that morning, and whatever the enemy tried to do, we were ready because "we have rank" The choir prepared in prayer and we were gearing up for a life-changing encounter! As we took the stage around 10am, to minister about three fast tempo songs we suddenly realized that there was no presence, no glory, or even a sense of feeling that God was about to show up. So we continued into our slow tempo songs, praying that God would make His arrival anytime soon....

At about 11:15, there was still no God, no break in the atmosphere, no nothing! Pastor took the platform with urgency in his eyes saying...this devil must be crazy! Pastor stood up and said these very words " I know who I am in the spirit, and I exercise my rank and authority as the Shepard of this house and I take control of the atmosphere in the Name of Jesus!" Immediately we felt an earthquake in the house and the place went up in a ridiculous praise!

During our re-cap meeting, we asked, what happen to where we sang for an hour, and nothing broke, but you got up and in about two minutes the house went up in smoke? The answer was really simple...Pastor stated these words..."the devil just wanted to check the rank"! I was like super-floored!! So I said that to say this, there is no (i) in team. We are all needed when it comes to fulfilling the assignment for that particular encounter.

Please allow this story to be a lesson to Pastors as well. You can't sit in the office until its time to preach, then fuss at the worship ministry to scorn because the house is not set when you get up.

A lot of times it's not that the worship team hasn't spiritually prepared, it's the fact that the enemy knows that your not coming out of the office, so he plans a field day for that worship service. Please be mindful leaders, that you play a very important role in praise and worship, sometimes just the assurance of your presence lets the novice worship leader know that I'm not out here alone, not only do I have God using me, if I mess up, I have my leaders ready to rescue me. "smile"

First of all let us understand the original intent for affirmation before we understand how it's being abused.

Affirmation is the act or an instance of affirming; state of being affirmed. the assertion that something exists or is true. something that is affirmed; a statement or proposition that is declared to be true. confirmation or ratification of the truth or validity of a prior judgment, decision, etc. *Law* . a solemn declaration accepted instead of a statement under oath. ***Affirmation was never meant to serve as an ego booster.***

When you find people that serve in ministry that don't like to serve unless their name is being called, you are dealing with a deceitful passion. It is NOT the job of the leader to spend every Sunday calling names. Yes, we are in full support of appreciating servants of the house of the Lord, but if that becomes your motivating factor, then God gets no glory. There are some people that act as if it is mandatory that their names be called. The danger of dealing with people with misplaced passions is that it's contagious!

That foul spirit will spread throughout your congregation and the next thing you know, you have a church full of people with a list of demands. The devil is a liar! Ministry is serving and serving is a privilege.

It is an honor to serve in the house of God! Don't allow people with negative spirits to sow seeds of deceit into your spirit concerning what they feel should be going on. Listen out for people that continuously say these words "if it was my church" or "God showed me" or "Pastor should have done it this way" . Through this spirit chaos and confusion is birthed as that individual not only "steals the spotlight" but take God's glory.

Pastors and Spiritual Leaders must be careful yet, selective now more than ever who is placed over God's people. My spiritual mother Prophetess Janet Floyd said to me once, "Andy, just like God anoints people, the devil anoints people!" The enemy will send in what you consider to be an asset to the ministry because of their tongues, extensive resume, and biblical knowledge.

However, the true test of a son or daughter is when they can receive rebuke and never miss a beat.

I am grateful to say that I haven't had 15 pastors in my life. There are literally spiritual bastards running around with a church resume as long as a restaurant menu. Their membership extends beyond the parameters of the city and they can boast that they have been part of almost every church in town. As soon as the leaders release the rod of correction...they are gone again! They are never satisfied, always finding something wrong with the way things are done, and always have an "idea" masked behind the name - vision. The ironic piece to this puzzle is that they are not faithful tithers, don't come to prayer, they are ministers with no association with the ministries of outreach in your church.

You might be wondering what does that to do with misplaced passions, let us dig even deeper to see. There will always be a time for ministry, the harvest is plenteous but the laborers are few according to Matthews 9:37.

We must be mindful of our motives behind serving in ministry. People are not going to come up and tell you, I'm only here to get my license and then I'm going to start my own church. Yet, all things work together for our good.

We must get back to the original plan that God created the church for. His plan was to redeem man and save souls from dying and going to hell. We focus so much on ourselves, _our_ issues, _our_ problems, and ministries, that we forget that we haven't won not one soul to Christ this year. We have become so busy trying to make sure we have engagements and first class airline tickets, we pass by someone hungry in the airport but because we're running late, we bypass the opportunity to change a life trying to get to a conference.

Have you ever notice that the conferences that we minister at are full of re-churched people"? The people that attend these events are coming for three reasons" to get another spiritual high, make a network connection, or find a husband or wife. The intentions are not to receive empowerment. What happens after the conference or "holy" convocation is over? The Spirit of God spoke something to me that ignited the fear of the Lord in me. He said, "my

people are not having conferences, revivals, and convocations for an outpouring of my spirit, they are simply having campaigns.

When my glory shows up, so does judgment. Therefore, the church is doing everything in its power not to invite my glory in the room, because when I come, I bring order."

God wants to do something major for the Body of Christ as a whole, but we are not allowing Him to because number one we are afraid of the David's' that may replace us.

As worship leaders and artists, we must understand the principle that to everything there is a season. Many of us are afraid that our season in the "limelight" may be up. So we pursue what is next on our agenda (not God's), the next thing that will keep us afloat – The Pastorate. Worship Leaders are moving into a position or calling they were not pre-destined, ordained or even anointed to do. The Pastorate is not an office to "try-out" – souls are at stake here. We are starting these churches because of the needs of mankind, deceiving God's people and ourselves simply because we need a cushion. What happens when you're not on the billboards anymore or the engagement requests have decreased? God said he would give us Pastors after his own heart. His intentions were not meant to be used as a substitute of the anointing or extra income. It is imperative that we know we are serving leaders with pure and Godly motives.

A Church Is No Stronger Than It's Leader

We hear a lot of people today saying that they are called to lead worship because they can sing.

This phenomenon has gripped the hearts of 'worship leaders' nationwide, but are you able to give time to consecration and prayer? There is a serious price that comes with being called to the ministry of worship. You must FIRST deny yourself, ensuring that you are not only a team player but able to keep an open line of communication between your leader and the members of the team.

Leading worship is not just singing on Sundays and telling people what to play and do. Your life should be an example of holy living. Remember, you are a beacon of light for successful and effective worship. We are living in the last days and Jesus is soon to return. No man knows the day nor the hour when the son of man shall appear, we were charged with being sure that we are ready.

Our lives here on the earth are supposed to exemplify a greater testimony that our God reigns with wisdom and strength.

My encouragement to you today is to allow God to affirm your ministry, and your leaders will follow. Running out as a wild buck on the loose trying to prove that you've been called to the music ministry is not necessary. Exemplify the heart of a servant through submission. Submit! Submit! Submit!

CHAPTER SIX
AWAKENING THE WORSHIP LEADER
IN YOU

The healing process begins when you decide that you will no longer be held captive to the bondages of Satan. Through this process you must make up in your mind that where you are is not where you want to be. This allows God to re-establish and revive your passion for worship. You will undoubtedly know when God has begun to work on you because the first thing that will change is your sound! Sound? Yes *sound!*

As a worship leader and prophetic psalmist, my biggest and most fulfilling joy is being able to lead Gods people into a tangible glory. A glory so thick that lives have no other choice but to be changed! A charged atmosphere is the breeding ground for miracles.

Every opportunity you are afforded to stand before God's people should be cherished. I love worship! I love seeing the people of God getting their needs met and God being glorified. When we enter the realm of worship, our petty situations and circumstances cease to exist because our hearts are opened to what God wants to do through us.

Worship takes us to a place in the spirit where flesh truly dies and the spirit on the inside of us takes it's rightful place. In the ministry of praise and worship I have found some key elements that have helped me in my ministry over the years. Many people have asked me, how do you effectively bring into subjection every atmosphere that you stand in? As worship leaders there are some strategies that are available to help music ministries across the country prepare the way of the Lord. It is very important to always have a goal preset for your encounter. That goal typically comes through communication with the Leaders of the church.

What are you looking to accomplish? What type of event is it and what is the vision behind that event? What did God say would be the outcome of that event?

If you are a worship leader and you never consult with the Pastors to see where God wants to take the atmosphere that day, start doing it. It doesn't matter how anointed you are, and how many recordings you have done, you will never see more for the house than the Pastors. I'm not saying that you don't ever grow to a place to where you don't know the spirit of the house, but if you are hitting and missing during worship and the Pastor has to come and set the house for the move of God, there is a disconnect.

I have much respect for worshipers who are capable of pulling the best out of the Leader because of the thickness of glory that rest in the house. Don't ever get to a point where you are so knowledgeable, you are too high for your own good.

In the next couple of pages I will share with you worship leaders whether novices or experienced, some keys that will help you bring the Glory of God in a very powerful way. Let's go!

Effective Keys For Worship Leading

- *Preparation*

The number one key to effective in worship leading is being prepared. Preparation is not limited to a song list contrary to popular beliefs. Preparation actually begins as soon as the worship service is over that prior week. One of my spiritual mentors gave me this quote and I teach it everywhere I go and it is the 5 P's!

P- Proper

P- Preparation

P- Prevents

P- Poor

P- Performance

It is mandatory that you take this particular part of the ministry very seriously, because whether you believe it or not, the deliverance that is needed for that man, woman, boy or girl depends on your ability to be mature enough to prepare for the worship encounter. There is nothing worse than a person trying to lead you into place that they have never been before.

It is okay to say you don't know what to do in certain situations. Would you want a novice doctor performing open heart surgery on you? The people of God don't come to church for experiments, but for breakthrough! Therefore, worship leaders, band, and vocalists alike, never be caught unprepared!

- *Clarity In The Spirit*

Now this is a kind of touchy subject to speak on because in reality, do you ever get to a place where you know what God is going to do all the time? No! If that was the case, you would be Omniscient.

Yet, there exists a place in God where you will receive clear instructions. So, you may be wondering, if that is the case Psalmist, why do we hit and miss the mark? I'll explain...

In any worship experience there are 3 types of anointing that are in operation.

They are:
1. The <u>Levitical</u> Anointing
2. The <u>Judah</u> Anointing
3. The <u>David</u> Anointing

Whether you allow them to fully operate or not is your call. Clarity is simply the understanding of knowing what is supposed to be. You must be able to submit your will to God's will and allow yourself to be an instrument for the purpose of God. If this does not happen then the worship encounter becomes another service, entertainment and/or parading of flesh in God's sight.

The body of Christ has enough entertainers within the industry. We need the glory, we are desperate for the glory and his people are crying out for it. Now is the time for the true remnant worshippers to arise, stand and be counted for.

The Levitical Anointing is found in operation in Deuteronomy 5. In this chapter we find a clear example of knowing and understanding the rank in the spirit where Moses was the spokesperson for the people.

The problem we have in the church today is so many worship leaders want to be stars and celebrities. There are some places in the spirit where even God only recognizes rank. The enemy has a field day in our worship service because we have unconsecrated worship leaders trying to operate in an illegal realm in the spirit. Just as with the seven sons of Sceva in Acts 19, the enemy is beating up on worshipers for not being prepared and having clarity of the assignment that has been given to their hands.

It is simple, stay in your lane. If you know you are not prepared mentally, spiritually, and physically to do warfare on behalf of an entire atmosphere, I urge you to immediately pass the mantle on. This is a pivotal turn that must take place.

The Levitical Priesthood was set in order for a reason. Their purpose is to train and equip us for the next level in our assignment. The worship leader is not the Pastor. It doesn't matter how close they are, the assignment is different. Therefore worship leaders, if you find yourself in a place where you are unfamiliar in the spiritual realm, don't just play around up there...get to a destination!

<u>The Judah Anointing</u> is a teamwork anointing! This is where to team as a whole plays a vital part in the intensity of the encounter.

There are many cases where the worship team sometimes fail as a whole, but there are also times where the anointing falls because of the UNITY!

Unity is the ability to do the same thing, for the same reason, the same way. A lot of teams cannot master unity in the spirit cause we have trouble mastering unity in the natural. If the worship director says that we are wearing "black skirts and white tops"…we are so saved we wear what we want but it's out of unity. There is not a person in the music department at your local church that is above correction. Sometimes as directors of these ministries, you have to make the word come alive in your department. The bible backs you up in *1 Timothy 5:20 –Them that sin rebuke before all, that others also may fear.* Just Joking!

But seriously, you must maintain order in the natural before you can require order in the spirit. To obtain the glory for the encounter that's needed for the people of God, we must work together. The team is no stronger than its leader. You can't be going off in your own world in the worship service saying that "it was the spirit"! Many people mistake that order for control. The worship leader is not trying to control your praise, but it is vitally important that nothing aggravates the Spirit of God. Pastor Benny Hinn says it to his team all the time "if He leaves it's your fault!" Which means, whatever sounds comes over the microphone that is not of God, you are risking the chance of losing the atmosphere. Be very careful when you allow too many operations to take place at the same time. There is a such thing called ONE SOUND! The objective of praise and worship is to create a mating ground for miracles.

When God is invited into a room full of expectancy, anything can and will happen!

The healing you need for your own life will manifest when Heaven kisses Earth. Start today seeking God for your next assignment. When you receive instructions from the Spirit of God, that is a sign that He has a set plan in motion for the encounter. FOLLOW THEM! There is a sound that brings God to attention, and that sound is praise.

He loves praise so much, that He created a whole earth just to get it. He loves, lives, and requires it. If there was ever a time when our worship leaders, minstrels, and singers needed to lay before God, that time is now. There is an end-time revival that is about to take place and the scenery of the Kingdom as you know it is changing. God is getting ready to unleash a fresh string of consecrated servants from the backside of the desert.

I don't know about you, but I just want to be available to God in any way He sees fit to use me. The strength of your worship team is not in the numbers, it's in the obedience. It doesn't take a large group of people to invoke the glory, only a holy group of people. Holiness is a LIFESTYLE! Everywhere you go, the world should be able to tell that there is something different about you.

Worship Leaders: Don't allow your team to even stand before God's people if there is no unity. If you have been made aware of issues between the team, and you refuse to deal with it before the time to minister, you are just as guilty. You are responsible for everything that goes into the atmosphere from the ministry of music. It is your job to live your life as an example. That is very rare these days, because 60% of our worship leaders want to be accepted in the in-crowd. I can't lead you and be your friend at the same time. Why? Because the first time you get out of line, and I check you on it, then you want to play the friendship card, and spread discord among the fellow team members and kill my integrity.

There has to be a certain level of respect for the office itself. If your team does not respect you, they will not trust you to lead them into the presence of the Lord. If your local congregation doesn't respect you, you are in trouble. I don't care how lonely you get, make sure at all times that your hands are clean. Preach unity until you're blue in the face, because where there is unity, THERE IS STRENGTH.

The David Anointing – This is by far the most misunderstood, misrepresented, and misplaced anointing in the Body of Christ today. Instead of speaking from a general observation only, I'll give you a double-header and share my personal experience to make this subject come to a clearer light.

In order to gain a clearer understanding of the power of the minstrel, let's take a look at the relationship between Saul and David. I must admit that when it was time to research and study this story, I literally had to repent because of the conviction it brought. Before we can deal with David having an anointing to play away evil spirits from Saul, let's travel together and find out why it was even needed.

In 1 Samuel 15 we see the anointing of King Saul, and very clear instructions given for the assignment through Samuel. God sent the word to Saul to go to war against Amalek for coming up against Israel. The instructions were very simple, God said, KILL EVERYTHING!

How many times has God instructed us to deal with certain issues in our life that we continually ignore? *I believe God only deals with us openly after He has made multiple attempts to deal with us privately.*

It is vitally important as musicians and minstrels that we take our ministry seriously. I don't have to remind you the important role you play in the service. There are avenues that only minstrels can use to shift the atmosphere. It doesn't matter how anointed the worship leader is, how powerful the preacher is, music is a principle sound that offers a principle affect. Saul didn't call for a prophet or evangelist. Even in the midst of Saul being disobedient to God and being tormented by God on a consistent basis, he understood the power of the yoke-destroying anointing.

Our 21st century churches are full of 5-6 piece bands, but are we operating in demonstration and power? A lot of people confused skills and gifts with anointing.

The bible declares *in Psalms 33:3 "Sing unto a new song, play skillfully with a loud noise".* Skillful singing and playing is a must as it is time out for allowing people to practice on atmospheres.

God is a God of order and there is only one type of sound He will accept and that sound has to be purified and uncontaminated. A lot of minstrels are offering up a foul sound to God and He is rejecting it. *"I don't want that ...God says!" I don't want your way of doing things!* The word declares that God is a spirit and they that worship Him, MUST worship Him in spirit and in truth.

Can you imagine what will happen in your church if your minstrels completely surrendered to the mighty hand of God? Can you imagine the glory that would release in every encounter? God told me in 2010, "as much glory as you want, is as much glory I can give, cause I will never run out and you will never experience the same glory twice." What aword! I don't know about you, but I want the glory!

I want so much glory that, when I sit at the organ, the enemy becomes very afraid, because he knows that I have a consistent track record of tapping the glory realm of the spirit. That is why everything that plays a part of the worship encounter is important.

Today, begin setting yourself apart so that God can use you. You have been chosen for such a time as this. Walk in that anointing! Walk in that power not allowing anyone to make you settle for anything less than the glory. God is preparing you at this very moment for your day of exposure! It takes power to change lives, and God has given you everything you need pertaining to life and godliness. So be encouraged and know that out of your life God will get the glory. Say Amen!

ACKNOWLEDGEMENTS

First to my Lord and Savior Jesus Christ, He alone is The Author and Finisher of my faith!

To my family, who continues to remind me that "The Best Is Yet to Come"

To my mom, "Theresa", my biggest critic and supporter! I am grateful to have an example of a survivor.

My loving grandmother, Alice Richards, thanks for fighting for me!

To my Godparents, LaDonald and Marcia Ensley, Your example of true holiness and dedication to ministry has yielded this fruit in return.

To my brothers and sisters: Fred Smith Sr., Anthony, Steven, Pastor Fred (Ashley), Tamara, Janiyah, Cordell, Brittany, and Mitchell...thanks for all of the support and prayers!

To my Spiritual Mother, Dr. Janet Floyd, if it was not for you, I wouldn't have known that I could succeed in life, attain my destiny and fulfill my purpose. Hearing the repeated words of me being second to none provoked me to go after my dreams, and for that I will forever love you. I appreciate every second you are continuously calling my name out in 5:00 A.M. prayer..."say yes"!

To My Spiritual Leaders and greatest Pastors in the nation, Bishop Danny & Dr. Carolyn Hunt, thank you for showing me a more excellent way, I thought I knew excellence in ministry until I made it to you guys! Keep birthing out and the return will be greater than you could ever imagine. To the best church in the world Walk In The Word Family Church, love you guys so much for your support and prayers!

To My Grandparents in Ministry, Superintendent Billy and Missionary Lena Caldwell, you all have been there for me in ways no one else has, thank you for all of the training and teaching me the most valuable lesson, how to be and stay humble. Love you and the Lighthouse and Dubach COGIC.

To the best friends a person can ever ask for, Mario & Ariel Manning, thank you for being there, thank you for the encouragement and support. To Jordan and Brandy West, you guys rock!

I am eternally grateful for the favor God has given me that allowed Dr. Judith McAllister to write the foreword on my first book. You are such a role model when it comes to the true essence of praise and worship.

To Pastor David Brinson, your ministry is pure and genuine and I'm grateful to call you my brother.

To Prophet Brian Carn and Prophetess Marcia Morrison, thank you so much for the opportunity to experience ministry on greater scale. I respect and honor the mantle that rest on your lives as well as the Kingdom connection God has given us, and I am forever grateful the prophetic mentors God has placed in my lives.

To Marita, honored to call you my sister!

To Bishop Rasby & Pastor Jaqueline Mason and the Impact Churches Inc. You guys have literally pushed destiny out of me by encouraging me not to be afraid. Thank you for every open door that Full Gospel has afforded me to walk through.

To all of the Leaders and Pastors who have allowed me over the years to gain experience by opening doors for my ministry. Your support and love will never be forgotten.

To Dr. Gladys Blanson, {MY VERY FIRST PASTOR}, Dr. Rosemary Williams, Apostle Cornell & Patricia Hamilton, Bishop Larry & Pastor Wanda Brandon, Bishop Kelvin & Pastor Rhonda Stewart, Pastor Johnny and Pamela Drumgole, Bishop Michael Douglas & Lady Sonya, Pastor George & Lady Charlotte Cooper, Pastor Luther & Lady Andrea Black, Bishop Don & Pastor Sharlaski Banks Apostle Gilbert Wilson, Tehillah And The UICC Family thanks for the continual of Face 2 Face Ministries. May the Grace of God continue to cover your ministry.

To my father, Pastor Felix and Lady Joycelyn Williams, when God answers prayers, He answers them well, thank you for coming back into my life right when I needed you the most. Your wisdom and knowledge of the music ministry is priceless and I am glad I have a legacy to follow. Love you dude!

To Pastor Jason Nelson, Pastor Wosheka Burriel, President Duane Terry, & Pastor Trent Cory, it was my honor having you guys share in the momentous occasion with me. I cherish the anointing God has entrusted you with. To every Worship Leader, Minstrel, Musician, & Singer – Thank you for the support you have shown by purchasing this book. I declare over your life and ministry supernatural favor and increase. I am eagerly looking forward to the testimonies and praise reports that shall arise from around the country. No matter what, stay focused! Allow nothing to detour you from your Divine Destiny! I love you and know you are always in my prayers. We Are Better Together!

Faithfully yours,

Psalmist Andy D. Smith

CONTACT INFORMATION

Write to Us:

Andy Smith Ministries
P.O. Box 4623
Monroe, LA 71211

Phone: 800.311.4045

E-mail: asmithmonroe.com
Website: www.andysmithmonroe.com

Instagram, Periscope & Twitter: @AndySmithMonroe

Facebook: Facebook.com/AndySmithMonroe